WAKE UP BLACK MAN

Your Future Is Calling You

Written By

Duz Mack

WAKE UP
BLACK MAN
Your Future Is Calling You

Written By

Duz Mack

Edited By

Toni Crump

Mary Jefferson

Cover Designed By

Mylia Tiye Mal Jaza

WAKE UP BLACK MAN: Your Future Is Calling You

ISBN: 978-0-557-67853-2

Author/Publisher
Duz Mack
www.bepublished.biz
toni_crump@buildingfuturegenerations.org

Publisher of Record
Lulu Enterprises, Inc.
860 Aviation Parkway, Suite 300
Morrisville, NC 27560

Self-Publishing Associate
BePublished.Org
mari@bepublished.org

Dr. M.M. Jefferson
P.O. Box 8324
Jackson, MS 39284

First Edition
Printed in the United States of America.
Recycled paper encouraged.

TABLE OF CONTENTS

Introduction

I am writing this book to reach out and help change the way young Black men think. I believe that our young Black men think the way they do because no one has taken the time to tell them about the gift of freedom that was given to them on a silver platter. They never had to do anything for it except enjoy it. The average boy or girl of today doesn't have a clue that thousands died so they could vote and have the right to enjoy America to its fullest.

As young Black men and women, you did not just wake up one morning with the right to apply for a job at your favorite bank or your favorite law firm. Someone took your place on the firing line many years ago. Now, you have all these rights, but aren't doing anything with them.

So my goal today, and my message today, is to shake you and shake you until I wake you up from your sleep so I can tell you what time it is. Young Black man, right now while you are sleeping (and missing school and hanging out on street corners) someone is watching you and planning your future for you.

Society has already counted you out by asking you to miss one more day from school, sell one bag of dope, make $10,000 that you can't even put in the bank, and break into houses to steal other people's stuff. Today, if you choose to wake up, I will show you how to get your own stuff.

Number one, you are driving a $200 car but have $10,000 worth of wheels on it! My advice is that you sell the wheels, enroll in a local college, and then apply for a grant. When people see that you care about yourself, they will begin to care about you too. So wake up and take your future back from those that have counted you out.

Number two, there are two roads to the future – the one that the world has picked for you and the one that your mama and daddy fought for you to have (and that thousands around the world died for so you could have the American dream). Anything less than living the dream will be a slap in the face of them that bore the rough injustice in your place for you to be able to go to any school that you choose and get an education.

To make all of this happen, they came to one conclusion: no pain no gain. You see, they had already been told that they never could vote in any of the Southern states. So they got in agreement, knowing that if they tried to vote that their suffering and pain would be almost too hard to take. Instead of going with the flow, having you and your future on their minds, their quest for justice pushed them ahead to die if necessary and to be beaten over and over again.

They got knocked down and got up over and over again. They rooted in and out of the police firing line like pistons in a car motor. And yet, you have no scores. You see, all of this has been given to you freely. And to receive it, all you have to do is get back in school and educate yourself because, besides God, knowledge is the most powerful force in the universe.

So, don't worry about quick money. Just continue to educate yourself and long-term wealth will embrace you. You will see. When you begin to educate yourselves and hook up with each other, you all will become giants with information about your community and the world. And knowledge can bring you the wealth, but lack of it will produce poverty.

Chapter 1

God Is A Must, All Day and All Night

For us all, God is a must, all day and all night. Since we were made by God, for God's purpose, then it's only right for us to center our lives around His will for us. We should arise early in the morning with thanksgiving on our lips and in our hearts, and go to sleep at night with the same concept. In other words, we should put God first in everything that we do.

Education without God won't work or prosper. It may get you to a place of plenty, but your foundation will always be shaky. The blessings of God make money, and education reigns supreme in the land. So when you start your college career that the slaves made possible for you, inject God in it from the first day that you go, until your college career is over. And then, I want you to go out and throw out lifelines to those who are less fortunate than you. Tell them the story of how God was right there with you all the way.

By doing this, you will encourage many others to go back to school who thought for sure they had no hope left. When you tell a few thousand dropouts how God helped you to get back in school, and they become excited and tell a few thousands, we will begin to educate the whole neighborhood in city after city and town after town.

When people are encouraged in the right way, they will respond in a positive way. Leaving God out of your plans is like baking a cake without the ingredients, it will not rise. He is the only one that can stabilize a man's life, every move in your life. No matter how good you plan it, without God it will surely fail.

It is very dangerous to leave God out of your plans, after He has blessed you and carried you to the top. Now you are educated with plenty of land, big houses, big cars, and a big bank account. But if you leave God out, the Word of God tell us, you will surely perish and all that you struggled and worked so hard for will be laid up for the just.

But you may ask, "What is a *just* man?" A just man is someone that will remember that God is his source and God is the one that gave him the power to get wealth. An educated man will be called just because he will have enough money to buy 10 houses, but will only buy one and take the rest of the money and feed the poor. This is why so many of our superstar football players, basketball players and baseball players get rich quick and then end up broke so quick.

Athletes and celebrities also end up that way because they took their eyes off God and started looking at Hollywood and the other fashions of the world. You see? The people that made them rich, right from the beginning, had no plans to keep them rich. They dangle all this stuff in front of them and they become like condors. They piped all this momentum of wealth through them, at the end of their careers, most of them have nothing left. Well, nothing except worn out, knock-kneed bodies that are mentally damaged far more than you can see.

And at the end of their careers, they always ask, "How did this happen to me?" I say that the day you walked away from the things of God, the enemy sought you out to take you down. He knows that the blessings are in God and with those that stay with God. So, you see, the foundation that we build our career on must be God-rooted.

When I visited a certain big city not too long ago, my heart was hurt over our kids and their outlook on life. They are in a low place of thinking. But it's not too late! The time has come upon us with urgency. We must raise up the next generation of Black boys in the fear of God and break the curse that is rampaging among them. And after we have done this, we must flood every school and every college and every university in America with educated kids.

We must break the curse of being last in everything that God have given us, starting with our education. We must get up and step up and take our place at the top, which was why we were brought to America in the first place. We were and still are a strong generation of men. We cannot and will not be denied, when we take our place in the world, in our home, and on our job.

Yes, the world will take note when the newly-educated Black man comes on the scene with God on his side and blessings covering him. But, to make sure that this happens, we must hurry to the classroom and catch them at an early age. We can't wait on, or depend on, the teachers alone to educate them. We must pitch in on a daily basis.

It is very true that, if a tree is tied while it is bent over to the side, it will grow up crooked. But, if it is tied off straight, it will grow up straight. We must catch our kids at the age of one, and store in their minds – on a daily basis – that in their lives, God is first and education is second. We must let young Black boys know at an early age that you can't run with the pack. You must run ahead of the pack. The reason why is because the playing grounds are not level.

We must tell our kids the truth about the world and the people that have ruled over it. They must gear up and empower themselves at an early age, and they must be ready to compete on a world-class level at every age of their life. We need to let them know that they must be two times better than their counterparts before they are counted worthy.

That's why we have to have God in every plan that we make for ourselves.

You have to accept that racism and injustice have never been on vacation. They just went into a closet and dressed themselves up. But underneath that suit, all hell is still raging against the Black man. So, we must be sharp, quick and ready at all times, very watchful at all times, and ready to call everything wrong and unjust that has been done to us. But we must do it in love, or we sure will be just like them.

If they give us a lemon, we have to make lemonade out of it because love breaks barriers of racism, you know. As a matter fact, when White kids are first born, if no one tells them to treat Black people differently than they do White people, they never would know that there was a difference in people. Racism is not born in kids. Lowdown ways have to be taught to them. And to every parent that teaches their kids racist things, you will have to answer to God one day.

For as a mother, you have been put over them just as the father has also been put over them, but neither one of you owns them. God only loaned them to you so you could grow them up in his knowledge, and so they could spread the good news of Jesus Christ. That, my friends, is the only reason why children are born into this world. And when you decide to take them off that route, and put them on a route of hate and not of love, you have changed the plans of God and payday awaits you.

Chapter 2

The Plantation Sharecropper Family

The contents of this chapter have been locked away in my memories for decades. I never had plans to wake up the sleeping giant, until I was inspired by two of my grandchildren – my grandson, VJ, and my granddaughter, Toni.

Toni lives about 10 miles away from me. VJ lives with me. Every weekend, when VJ would go to Toni's house and play with her brother, every time he came back home I would ask him where Toni was. And for the hundredth time he gave me the same answer, "At home reading a book." By hearing this over and over, I began to listen with a great interest and told myself something. If Toni can read hundreds of books that were written by other people, maybe I can write a book telling my story and it can be read by hundreds of other people.

It starts from when I was a 2-year-old. My father moved his family to a plantation that was very promising, according to the information that was given to him by a certain source. This turned out to be very untrue, and my daddy realized after a little while that moving the family to the plantation was a very big mistake. First of all, the living conditions were horrible. We had no running water and no electricity, only lamplight.

The house itself was poorly built with no insulation, and cracks ran up and down and around the outside of the house. My mama would go to town and ask White folks for newspapers that they had read and magazines that they had left over. Now, we were too poor to buy a lot of glue. So my mama used Argo starch to glue the paper to the wall over the holes, so we could have some protection from the cold weather. I can still see her standing there, with white Argo starch running down her arms.

She was tired but she had to keep on working. The north wind came in the cracks like an air compressor was forcing it through. I mean, holes and cracks were everywhere. We could see the chickens under the house through the floor, and we could see the sun in the daytime and the stars at nighttime.

And, when it rained, we all got wet. We had buckets everywhere catching rainwater.

And to be plain, the true test was mind-boggling. We had no toilet! So, my daddy built a little house, about 4 ft x 5 ft, with wood handles on each side so we could pick it up and move it every four to five days. He would dig a hole about two feet wide and about three feet deep. There were so many of us that the house had to be moved often because it filled up very quickly. The little house sat right over the middle of the hole. Now we also did not have any toilet tissue, so we bagged up grass sacks full of cotton and used it for tissue.

But no matter what came his way, daddy was convinced that he was going to make it, because as far as he could see things, he was a man among men. So he stayed on at the plantation, trying to make the best of it. He worked very hard for pennies on the dollar for the rich plantation owner.

But at the end of each day, there was no thanks. The only thing that was said was go home, hush up, and shut up. Oh, and early tomorrow morning be ready to get up and do it again. That was the way it was for years. That way of talking has been handed down to us by the same people, those who had our parents in slavery.

My daddy was a kind man. He worked hard and gave a lot to everyone that crossed his path. You see, the way that daddy saw life was that there were only four things in life that a man needed. First was God, second was a good shotgun, third was a good pistol to keep bad people off you, and fourth was a good woman to love you and bear your children. That was as far as daddy could see things. And that type of thinking comes from people making you shut up and take what you get, and be happy about it.

While I was on vacation a few months ago, my own brother -- who was hosting our family reunion – was letting everyone talk a little bit about their family. When my turn came, I wanted to talk a little about the past, but I was told, "Okay, Lee, go sit down." Well, when he told me that, everyone in that room laughed. It was not funny to me.

All of our lives, that is what we have been told. That moment brought me back to my plantation roots. I can see why most of our kids have no idea who they are, all that they know is that they were born and that they live. So when I digested that in, I thought about the fact that I am not a take-what-you-give-me man. "I am not like daddy, who saw only four things for himself that he needed in life." All that he picked was good and he was on the right track, but no one had the right to stop him from dreaming. I believe that everything that a man envisions for himself and sees for himself, he can have.

God has allowed me to tell my story more on the next few pages of this chapter. I will be free on every page to tell the story of the plantation sharecropper family and no one can hush me up, shut me up, or hurry me up. I will rise up with a mighty pen in my hand, and tell the plantation story of the past that got us to the point and place where we are today.

My daddy worked many hours each day because that was what the White boss expected from sharecroppers. We stayed on his place, and he was supposed to get half of everything that we were supposed to work for. However, it never came out that way.

You see, when we first started sharecropping, the owner loaned my daddy the money to buy all of his seed, fertilizer, cotton, and corn spray to kill insects. It cost so much that, no matter how much cotton and corn and peas we picked and pulled, at the end of the year we always were in the red. The landowner kept the books and fixed the books. At the end of every year at settlement time, which we were supposed to do and did do, the answer was always the same. He would tell my daddy, "I am sorry, Papa. But, you went in the hole again."

I got so tired of seeing my daddy crying and hurt. But he needed to stay in the house on the plantation, and the man was not treating him right. So, you can say that he was caught between a rock and a hard place. After years of abuse from the plantation owner, we were beginning to grow up. Once we were big enough to go to the field, daddy was able to get a break. Now, he only had a 3rd grade education, but after working for nothing for years, he finally got a vision for himself and his family.

He still wanted the first four things that he originally saw for himself (and many, many more things), but all of a sudden he began to dream. He was now moving quickly towards having plenty of experience. I heard him one day talking to my mother.

"The time has come for you and the kids to go to the field and farm," he said. "Pick cotton, pick peas and pull corn. But as for me, I am going to town and get a job so I can get us out of this mess. A man needs to feel like a man, so no more sharecropping. From now on, you and the kids will work by the hour for him. I got that point straight with him. No more borrowing from the old-time loan shark who kept our heads under water for decades."

But the abuse did not stop once daddy went to town to work. We started working by the hour. We made 30c per hour for chopping cotton, and we were supposed to make $15 per week. The problem was that we were told that $15 per week would come to 10 hours per day. Instead, we always worked more than 10 hour each day for the same money.

Depending on the way the sun rose and fell, some days we worked 18 hours and some days 16 hours. But almost every day, we worked from sun up to sun down yet he always called it 10 hours a day. The sun was our clock, at least the only one he went by. But we had one thing on our side that even the iron-fist-ruling, prejudiced farm owner could not control. It was unity. We had each other's back.

The way we saw it back then was that all we had as people was each other. We were not scattered all over the place, meaning every man is for himself. We were raised in a community and we had love for each other. It was one for all and all for one.

The one thing that made the KKK hate us so much in the past was the one thing that we did better than any one else back then – the ability to unite and organize. You see, you don't have to do anything to me, but do something to one of my brothers and I will be angrier than he will be. That was the way that we lived on the plantation. If my mama killed a hog or a cow, everyone in the neighborhood got a little piece. And next month when someone else killed one, she got a little piece.

By everyone in the neighborhood giving each other a little bit every week and every month, we all got through the year in spite of the evil cotton plantation owner. And now, looking back at the past, I can see the future for us and it will be a bright one for us if we take the right path into it. First, we must go back to the old landmark when every man and woman and child in the neighborhood was important.

Now, we have gone our own way and every man is for himself. No one cares about the neighborhood anymore. In the past, every day my dad would show his concern for his kids and the people that lived around them. At suppertime, he would question you about your day and every thing that you did that day. It will be very easy to catch something that is out of the normal, if your kids are checked on a regular basis. And by doing this, you would know if the gang is trying to get to them or if they themselves were dreaming of a way to commit or carry out a bad act.

A neighborhood doesn't just stop loving itself for no reason. It happens because we parents stopped carrying the torch of love. We must stop and turn around, and pick it up again and hold it up high as we carry it. Our kids need to see the world, and each other, the right way again. We have to keep on loving each other. It is the key to keeping people together.

In the past, we only had a little but, when we put it all together, we lived like we had a lot. Everyone in the neighborhood was full and fit. Today, we have a lot and live like we have a little. The reason is because we as Black people have listened to other people's ideas and decided to go it alone in the world. By doing this, we have let the spirit of jealousy in.

We have decided that, "I got mine and you better get yours." There is no more, "What about the little old lady that we had been tucking in at night, and the little old man that we used to help across the street?"

Now, we will take another route so our paths don't meet up with a neighbor's. It goes on and on in our neighborhood. We are getting off track in everything that made us great in the first place, and that was unity. Listen to me. In good times and bad times, our chances are always better when we stand united.

As Black people, we sure should act and be smarter than a lion. You see, a hungry lion can't read but has common sense. He knows that, if he can scatter and split the herd, his chances of getting and killing a calf would be better. But when all the bulls and cows are all bound together in a tight mold, the lion won't eat the calf. It is as simple as that.

It's the same concept for Black people. When a Black man declares to the world that he is rich and self-made, and shows the Black race that he is pulling away from them, the normal thing will happen. Sooner or later, he will make a mistake in his life. When he does, the world will be watching and he alone will pay. But when we team up like the zebras, we can't be stopped.

See, there may be a million zebras in one herd and every one has stripes. But when they team up, every one of them runs different ways, kick all over the place, and they no longer look like a single zebra. They look like one big force coming at you. And when we get like that, the world will take notice. When they realize that we are not alone anymore, that we care about each other and notice whether or not one of us is hurt, they will take notice.

The time has come when we must stop snitching, selling each other out, and back stabbing each other. Back on the plantation, there was always a handful of people that would not join us in our quest for justice and equal rights. They had been either bought out or sold out. That trend is still going on today.

Back then, all that the boss wanted to know was who among us was the greediest or the most ignorant. Then he would give him a penny or two more than the rest of them made. That one would then snitch and tell every move of all of the rest of the people. Back then, we called them houseboys (if you know what I mean).

As a people, we have become like an atom splitting itself apart violently, and we can't let that be. We must put back together what our enemy has set up and tricked us into tearing apart. We who know the truth must work the truth back into its rightful place. No one is going to help us. The world is watching us and laughing at us, and hoping that we keep on tearing each other apart and setting up roadblocks for each other.

They can't get us down on their own. That's why they always use another Black man to do the dirty work like the houseboy, the smoke of the Black family. But the few of our own that have been selling us out for years will not be strong enough to stop us when we team up. With power like the great waterfall or the Mississippi River, we won't be stopped until our people get their minds back and start thinking again!

We are not letting, or going to take, anyone's word for what is good for us anymore. From now on, we are going to read every book and double check our homework. We are going to eliminate the slip-up that has been used to count us out far too long. Some of our people failed by this all were educated – like doctors, lawyers, schoolteachers and other people that were of importance to the Black race –

and then something happened to them. Maybe they got fired or sick or something.

What happened is not important. What is important are the true facts. The Black race was split up and was not there when they needed them. Some of them went under the bridge, and some of them went into the alley to get high and to forget it all. And the same kind of needle some of our doctors used to heal people, they are now using them to kill themselves with poison.

We can no longer stand on the corner and let this keep happening. We must act and act now. And we need to be there for them. What's more important is that our youth that are coming on now are learning from us all. We need our whole race to come together and stay together. In unity, we are unstoppable.

Chapter 3

Ignorance is the Black Man Number One Enemy

When I think about how little it is that we know, versus how much we don't know as Black men, it scares me. The world is evolving around us, and certain races and certain groups of people in it are getting richer and richer. What I mean is that, most of the races of people in America are all in line for their piece of the American dream. But at an alarming rate, a great percentage of Black men are still not applying for what the world has in store for people like CEO's of major companies and presidents of top universities.

The reason why this is happening is because we are still depending on other people to read the newspaper for us. We trust them to tell us the truth about what is in it. If we are going to change this trend of being last in everything, we are going to have to step up and do our own homework. We are failing in life because we are letting someone else keep the scoreboard for us. Understand that the playing grounds have never been fair. We have always been asked to run one-sided races. We have to dig deep and search hard.

We have to learn what others are going to know before they learn it. We know this from the last 100 years or more. We have consistently been asked to catch up or work harder than others over and over. It's like we have been asked to go to the race and get on the starting line in Florida, but our counterparts go to Memphis and get on the starting line. The rules seem like they are set like this: We all must start at the same time and drive the same speed limit. But the hard part is, in order to be counted by the checkered flag, we all must be in the same place on the same day and at the same time – which is Chicago.

Black people have a tough chin, and we can put the proof in the pudding. This is because we have been set back, kicked back, and asked to stay back for so long and by so many. However, when it is to their benefit, we have been ordered to come back and get in line for whatever is being cooked up for

Black folks. I am saying that the things we don't know as Black men have kept us down. This has lasted for generations. That is plain laziness and plain ignorant.

But my hope today is that after Black men finish reading this book, they will rise up and start thinking like the determined fishermen. The true determined fisherman went to the lake one day to do what he loved best, which was fishing. As soon as he sat down, he got a little nibble and he grabbed his pole. He pulled it up and saw one of the biggest fish that he had ever seen. But, the fish got off the hook and dropped back in the water. Determined to catch the fish, the man sat there all day.

When he got home, he told all of his friends about what he had seen and they all laughed at him. The truth was that he had seen the fish and he was satisfied with the evidence that he knew the fish was truly there. He made up his mind that if it took 1,000 trips to the lake, he was going to catch that fish. The key thing was that he kept on going and he kept on going. Then, after many trips, he finally came home one day with the monster lying in the back of his truck. The true fisherman story is no different from our daily struggle.

We have seen the mountain of wealth circulating around us every day. You see, wealth comes from different directions in life. Like a mighty bear at a waterfall catching salmon, we have to find out who has the wealth, who is seeing it out, and what are the qualifications for this job or that job, or that partnership (whatever the case may be).

We must qualify ourselves, then go out and position ourselves in the line of the wealth with mighty, intense searching – and wait for a signal. The way that we position ourselves is by having and acquiring knowledge. Knowledge is so real and so powerful that it can help us to gain it all, or be caught without it and lose it all. Right now I am thinking of someone who had the lack of knowledge in his life and it almost cost him everything that he loved.

This man had a daughter he enrolled in a very expensive and very prestigious college. Back home, he had a farm and nice house that were also expensive. He wanted his daughter educated with the best. So, he worked two jobs to keep her in school. Finally, after months of hard work, he could no longer keep it up without breaking himself down. So with tears in his eyes, he called his daughter to his room and told her. He said he did not know for sure, but he might have to ask her to sit out of school for the rest of the year.

Well, by that time, his daughter had met and gotten to know a little farm girl who was very friendly with her. They had begun to talk every day. While they were talking at the lunch table one day, she told her little friends about her problem. She said she may have to drop out of school for a while because there were not enough finances to send her there any longer. The little girl told her to look around, and said that the school is full of White kids and only a hand full of Black.

She said, "All the Black kids have the same problem that you have, the lack of knowledge."

She said everyone else's parents went out and found grant writers, and they all go to school on grant money. When she heard that, she and her father got to digging and searching (and finding money). From that day on, no one in their family paid for college anymore. And that's the way we should be.

You see that little girl was in a good position. Her grades were good and she was not worried about money. Because all of her needs were met, she also had a heart of giving. When she saw that someone around her was in need, she was glad to point them in the direction of help if she could not help them herself.

That is the same way that we are supposed to be. As I look around at the condition that we are in, I can truly see what we need to do about it. We have to come to a place of plenty in our lives, where we are stable and no longer needing help, and begin to start to reach out and help others in need. We need to be just like that little girl. When someone comes across our path and needs help, we should always be well equipped to help them. We should always be able to give them a spiritual word of knowledge or give them a token of help in their hands. But this won’t happen as long as we stay in the same old frame of mind that we have now about the system.

We have to get up off our do-nothing behinds and do something about depending on other people and their system. Welfare and other programs like welfare have crippled the Black race, both women and men. It's taken away many people's self-esteem and survival skills, and now no one on it wants to work. It has made people very lackadaisical. It only should be for the elderly people that have worked all their lives, and the sick and needy.

The whole thing is off track for some women who get food stamps and other assistance, who also have a non-working man hanging around the house (using up the goods that the kids should get). He plays her, the kids, and the system. And it's all because he is lazy. Once a man becomes lazy, ignorance automatically sets in because they run side by side.

It's like getting a cold. Once you have it, a runny nose automatically sets in. Once a man becomes ignorant, he stops thinking for himself and starts accepting whatever idea he can get from any other means. But getting information from other people is always risky, because you really don't know who is truly on your side and has your back in love and life.

So you better get up and do your own searching to figure out what is best for your life, and for your wife if you decide that you want to be married one day. But I can tell you right now that if you keep entertaining laziness and won't get up off your do-nothing behind and do something, you continue to embrace ignorance.

No daddy that has raised his daughter to high standards will be willing to walk her down the aisle and give her to you, because you will be a misfit. You see? Laziness and ignorance will take you on a losing path a lot farther away than you want to go, and it will keep you there a lot longer than you want to stay. See, when you get on a path of laziness and ignorance, you will begin to do everything out of the normal.

Back in the day, people used to raise a lot of hogs and put them in a common fence. The hogs would not try to get out because, at the end of their nose, the farmer would put steel hoops in about three or four places. Now the hog could not stop what was being done to him because he belongs to the farmer and was not free. But you, Black men, were in bondage and now have been set free from slavery, yet you choose to still be in bondage. The farmer holds down the pig and puts steel hooks in his nose, but you have rung yourself out like a hog due to ignorance.

You have pierced your lard, your lips, and your belly navel and tongue – then call it the style. The real truth is that you are a plain, ignorant man. You have dropped your pants as low as a toad, and now your hands are not free because you have to use them to hold your pants up so you can get across the street. The very people you are going to have to go up against to get a world-class job are laughing at you. They're rolling on the floor because they know you will never be a threat to them in the condition that you are in right now. They also know that there isn't a single job, or person, that is going to give you a chance as long as you are on the level that you are on – which is a very low, and out of order and place.

But if you want to stop people from laughing at you and begin to get worried about competing against you, you have to get up and pump your mind up (all the way back into the winner’s circle of learning). Now it won't be easy, but your future is worth every bit of it. You see, there are only two types of people in the world: the losers and the winners, the ones that have it and the ones that don't have it. Most of the people that don't have it, don't have it because they never did anything to try and get it. And the reason why they haven't done anything about not having it, is because they have been dancing and entertaining the spirit of laziness.

When you play with lazy thoughts, ignorance will always come in and play a part in your life. You don't have to invite ignorance in your life. Just choose to be lazy and you will automatically have him as a guest. Like I said before, ignorance and laziness run parallel with each other. You can't have one without the other. To tell the truth about it, ignorance and laziness have stripped the Black man of his right and his inheritance worldwide.

See, the upper class and educated races have always preyed on laziness and taken advantage of ignorance. And today, we see signs everywhere and proof that the world has raised the bar. And, is continuing to raise the bar on us. But every time that they raise the bar, we must educate ourselves to that level and beyond.

One day, they won't have any room to raise it. Then, and only then, will we be able to step across it. Until then, we have to eat, sleep and live in the educated mold -- daily training our minds without wavering. We know that one day we will have our say. One day, we will have our share in the corporate world and top jobs everywhere. We can't go back. We can't even entertain the thought of going back. But we must stop being ignorant and lazy, and educate ourselves because going back will be harder than finishing the course.

I remember, a long time ago, when I teamed up with a group of friends to swim across a certain powerful river. The first 100 feet of the bank was easy. But when we got in the middle of the river, the waves were very strong and raging. But as we looked back at the bank where we just swam from, we realized that it was just as long to go back as it was to keep on going and finish the course. So we kept on going, and we kept on pushing and we kept on pumping. And after working very hard, we finally made it to the other side.

Those kinds of experiences will make a man scratch out all of the negative in his life. So, I am telling Black men everywhere to scratch out all of the negative in their lives. Make a decision to use only positive words. I am going to make it. I can make it and I will make it. That kind of thinking will elevate you higher than an airplane can fly you. For, the way to stay ahead is to think ahead and reach ahead. All great athletes use the same concept.

When a great football player gets knocked down, the first thing that he does as soon as he hits the ground is set the ball forward. The same thing goes for us. When something happens in your life and causes you to fall, don't get with your so-called friends and smoke dope. Instead, reach out into life and grab hope and hold onto it. That way, right when you are falling, you will be thinking of a way to get up. Never plan on staying down.

If a lazy man gets knocked down, most of the time he will choose to stay down. And because a lazy man is also an ignorant man, the lazy part of him won't let him dig deep and search out the future for himself. He will just accept whatever someone tells him or gives him.

If he doesn't get up and do something about his life, that will be the way he will live, and that will be the way he will exist. He will never be able to help anyone in this life, but will live his whole life in need himself. And it all will be because he was lazy and ignorant, and refused to get up and do something about it.

Chapter 4

The Stay-Home Dad

The stay-home dad is the worst dad in the world. But time is running out on stay-at-home dads because moms all across the world are getting tired. You see, God has always put the man in the front seat to take on the daily pressures of life instead of his wife. The woman is supposed to have the babies, and the man's job is take care of them. The woman's job is to stand by her man and not in front of him.

The only time a woman is to be out front is when the man has a setback, such as sickness or a lay off. And if you get sick, as soon as you are able you should take back your responsibilities instead of leaving your wife out there. If you get laid off, you should leave your job that day and look for another job the same day. You should never go home and become a chair potato, because boys watch what their fathers do. It is not good for a boy to see his daddy lying around on the couch at home instead of going to work.

But when he sees his dad getting up early every morning and going to work, it will leave a great impression on him. Because he sees his dad working and taking care of his family, he will grow up and take care of his family and believe that going to work every day is an honorable thing. The fact that you work every day and pay your way, and take care of your home, sends a great statement to your wife and kids that you care about them and you are there for them.

On the other hand, a stay-home dad that won't work but instead sends his wife into the workplace to earn their living is a disgrace to men everywhere. He can't lay it on the economy, because he did not work before the economy got bad. A lot of moms pet boys too much. When they grow up and get their own wife, they will be looking for the same thing. He will want to have everything given to him for free.

That's why a good father has got to be in the house as well. A woman is not a man. She cannot teach a boy how to be a man. She is soft by nature, and she was born that way. When a boy is around a woman too much, he will become soft and will not be able to lead other men. So we must make a decision to get up off the couch and step back into our position. We must take the pressure off of our wives, so we can be called men again.

And ladies, I am talking to you also. If you have a man at home that won't work, and you know that you are paying the bills, take heed. Tell him these things: get up and go to work, or get out permanently. Don't play with him about it. By you doing that, you just might save his future. Because once you put him out and hard times set in, he might do something about his life. But as long as you give free eggs, he will continue to suck them.

You see, it is very true that a man that won't work should not eat. Safe havens for the stay-home dad should be turned down. It should not be said about us, or among us, that we have big, Black lazy men at home watching TV while momma is out working. It is time for it to end.

A stay-home, lazy dad is like having two horses in the field that both eat the same amount of hay but only one of them is helping to pull the hay baler. Sooner or later, the hay baler will break. The same thing goes for you moms. If you continue to let that stay-home dad eat up and spend up everything that you and the kids have, sooner or later you all will starve. But if you make him get up and do his part, your boys will grow up knowing their role in life. They will be reasonable and will take care of their families, for you should never let a man out of his responsibilities when it comes to his family.

All across the country, kids are hurting and are in need of direction. That's why lazy, couch-dwelling, stay-at-home dads need to get up and get back in line to take their place in their children's lives as their leader. There are far too many bright minds going to waste because fathers won't get up, step up and do their part in their children's lives. Kids need to be influenced by someone who loves them. But if they can't, they will accept it from the world that doesn't love anyone.

Still, the world gets a great share of our children each day because their real dads won't get up and let their voices be heard while staying home and doing nothing. Too many fathers, working and non-working, are letting mom do the daddy part and the momma part in the house. By her taking on both parents' jobs, her struggle is really almost too hard to bear.

But if we could get all of the dads to get up and do their part in the upbringing of their kids, we could save millions or billions of dollars each year to help pave the way for kids that really need help. Every time a child goes wrong, it costs everybody. But every time a child goes straight, everybody wins. That is the reason why we have to keep on hammering away at non-working, stay-home dads. The fact is this, if you sleep with her and get a baby, you got a baby. And if you got a baby, you need to get up and do whatever is necessary to feed, take care of, and bring that baby up right.

You see, we all know that you got paid up front because you had fun getting the baby. Now, please be real and take pleasure in rearing him or her. You can't do that by staying at home and sitting on your do-nothing butt. The world is watching you and hoping that you will continue to stay right there on the couch, as you will never become a threat to them with that locale.

So you have to get up and stand out. Become a threat to anything and everything that will stand in the way of your family's well being. A non-educated child and worn-out mom are not matched for the new world. That's why you have to get up and do your part, like a real man does anyway.

It's just like when a logger loads his log truck. He will put so many logs on each wheel. It's called spreading the weight around. He knows that if he puts too much weight on one wheel, he will blow out a tire. The same thing goes for you, dad, when you get up and help mom. We call it sharing and spreading the responsibilities around between the two of you. But if you let mom do all the work, sooner or later she will burst something or blow out something.

Dad, if you get up and start saturating your child with support and good home training, the world won't be able to snare him or her. When a child has been fed and well taken care of, and a stranger comes along and tries to snare him with something of the world, he will remember his good parents and send the stranger on his way. If a stranger tries to tell your son or daughter of another way to success in life, other than the blessing of God and hard work, they won't listen to him.

So what I am saying to dads all across this country is that you need to get up and go into the working world. You need to help support your children so the world can't trap him or her. You know that the world will show your children a way to the top that will be quick-lived and damaging. The fast and quick way to the top is always the wrong way. The stable way to the top is all of us getting together, staying together, covering each other's back, and moving forward inch by inch.

Each time we go an inch, we must make an imprint and plant an anchor. That way, if we have to step back for a moment, we will have a solid rock to stand on. We know that we will get to the top, but not too fast. We want to take our time and get there slowly and for sure. On our way to the top, we will stop and plant ourselves solidly in every step. So from now on, we are going to take the farmer's approach in getting to the top of this game.

When a farmer experiences a drought for a very long time and suddenly gets a bit of rain, it may fall real fast and quick. If it falls with such force, it cannot be contained. It will run off the field just as fast as it fell down. But the farmer won't be fooled by it. He won't run out and put his precious seeds in the ground where the rain fell.

He knows that it did not penetrate the ground and go deep enough for his seeds to live and multiply. So, he waits for many days to go by. Finally, a long-lasting, slow rain comes and falls upon his land. Only after that will he put his expensive seed in the ground. The slow rain penetrated his ground deeply, and made it soft so that it lay open – waiting for the seeds to come and multiply themselves.

We are no different from the farmer. We know that waiting patiently and getting things right will reward us. When all of the stay-home dads get up, they can get their children qualified with their love and support is seen as they qualify themselves.

Black men, let’s stop accepting quick fixes. From now on, our goals will be long-term and stable.

Chapter 5

The Footprint of a Race of People on the Move

November 4, 2008, when all of the presidential votes were counted, something very awesome and powerful happened. A sign of the times was put on display for the world to see and judge when the word came down from the speaker that a Black man was going to be the "President of the United States of America." Like a mighty thunderstorm filled with lightning and rain, hope exploded all across the United States and the world.

Because of that, for thousands of years to come, every Black boy that is born in America will be told the story of how he has a chance to be president, or anything else that he wants to be. On that day, we decided not to be crabs. Instead, we got together and pushed one of our own out of the barrel so we all could have a chance to get out. Because of what we did, hope was branded in the minds of millions of Black boys. Like the print of a hot iron, it will never come out. People will teach it to their children and their children's children.

However, hope did not start the day that the president was elected. It started over 200 years ago. The old slaves sang about it in songs like "We Shall Overcome" and "If Anyone Makes It, Surely I Will." Now, they never thought that they would make it per se; but what they were singing about and talking about was their seed. You see, for generations and decades, we have been telling our young and upcoming kids that hope was in the air and, if they only believe and catch onto it, they will overcome anything. We have been moving towards the White House for more than 200 years, just like an inchworm steadily moving ahead.

The slave owners never saw it coming, but all of the slaves and old folks did. They sung the song right under his nose and he did not catch it. Every time he misused us, he inched us forward. Every time he raped one of our women, he inched us forward. But none of this abuse had to take place because he was basically getting free labor from the slaves. However, he didn't take into account all of the seed growing up and bearing fruit like their kind.

Being led by his quest to control everything in his eyesight and everything around him, the one thing that the slave owner couldn't resist the most was the Black slave woman. She was then, and still is to this day, packed with pure and uncut liquid sugar. A quality almost unmatched, and he knew this. Because of this quality he found in the Black slave woman, he kept on raping her and making babies. He didn't realize that his own seed would grow up one day and be humble like us, and would take almost anything for peace's sake.

That the part like him that thought like him would turn around and teach the rest of the slaves to think like a free man. What I am saying is that the slave owner bred the Black man out of slavery by having babies by Black women and abusing the Black men. His own seed grew up to think like him and wanted to be free like him! They would stop at nothing until they were free. And every time they did racial things to us, they inched us forward.

As a race of people, we have been on the move since every racial thing that has happened to us. The very thing that pushed us and kept us going forward was oppression and hope for a better life. The fact that Obama made it to the White House was easy to predict if you look at what's ahead for us. They are not going to let us off the hook because we are doing it right, no matter how hard we try. Look at what is happening now.

There are some that are never going to say that a Black man is good enough to lead. They had better wake up because we are on the move as leaders. We are beginning to teach millions of our youth to be world-class leaders. No matter how many times we are rejected, we will keep on returning until we get in and have a chance at the top in everything.

As football and basketball players, we are among the best. Yet, we hold a small percentage of the top jobs. That has to change. There is nothing wrong with being on the bottom as long as there is an honest road to the top that I am allowed to climb some day. That is the reason why we are tanking up on education and inching forward in every field known to man. It is going to take that to meet our next goal.

From now on, we will be like migratory birds that stop at many lakes on the way to the breeding grounds. No matter how many they stop at, they all have one thing in common – they will never consider any of the lakes home. They have their own breeding grounds and they won't settle for anything less. We must be the same way.

Now we know that there is nothing wrong with working at a clean up shop, or any other low-paying job. But in our minds, once and for all, we must remember that this is only a stop. It is very temporary and short, because my career is at the top. So today, I will work at the store; but tomorrow, I will own the store. Today I go to college, but tomorrow I will be the president of that college.

Today, I am calling all Black kids to begin their quest for higher learning. In return, you will line up for that great job because a good education will put you in line with that great job. So, starting today, I want you to take your mind and go into the wealth world. Put up a goal as high as the mind can think. Then, go back to school and get your education to begin to work your way all the way back to your goal.

Once you do this, showers of success will embrace you. The world thinks that the only thing that we do well is entertain others. That is right for some to a degree, but we are changing that for us in general. In the future, we will begin owning the hotels they have the events in. Ownership and education are friends. Stay in the education lane, and a good future will run upon you.

When you go out and educate yourself, the world might not like you but they can't deny you. Keep on moving and keep on inching forward. The future will be opening up for you. In your future, there will be many more first times for the Black man to rise to the plate. We have just begun to step up on the scene, and millions more are coming behind us. Some of them are presidents, lawyers, corporate heads, mall owners, heads of state, and every top position you can think of.

I am telling you that hope is in the air and the Black family is smiling again. If we don't make it now, it will be our own fault. We have proven to ourselves and to the world, over and over, that if we go to the door and no one answers, we will keep on coming back. We will keep on knocking and kicking, and screaming, until someone hears us.

Never again will we call injustice fair or right. We will call it out anywhere we see it. You see, the new hope that we have has now exploded all across the universe. It is bigger than anything that we ever had. It's like a new breath of life for our young people, and old ones too. So, while the air is rich with hope, we must capture the moment and lock in the winning attitude. We must not ever think about losing.

From now on, we will make a successful impact in our community and the world around us. We have been given a mandate to take our concerns and our goals to the next level. I know that progress has been made and that's good, but not good enough. We're still a low number of people going across the bridge where success is. We have to abolish our old way of thinking, tear down the old pathway, and put in a new roadway to hope.

From now on, hundreds of people will make it. And every once in a while, we must enlarge the road and super size the crossing so thousands of people can cross over into success on a regular basis. It's like when you go to the movies and stand in line. After you pay for your ticket, no one in the world has the right to tell you that you can't go in. As long as you have qualified yourself, you have a right.

Common sense tells us that our ancestors purchased our tickets over 200 years ago. History tells us they paid for it with pain and suffering. Yet, we have been paying on it since. So, as a people, don't ever tell us that we can't get in. Just ask us, "How may I help you get in the realm of success?" Because, like the great tectonic plate that turns the earth, we will always be coming and coming until we get in.

Chapter 6

What We Must Do When We Enter Into A Place of Plenty

When we enter into a place of plenty in our lives, we must rid ourselves of jealousy and selfishness. We have to be there for each other all the way. The greedy men of the world that have heaped up a great amount of the world's goods, really think that God made the world and put them in charge. But He never did such thing.

Look at it this way: if a blessed river runs by your house that is full of fish, all you need to do is catch your share of fish for your family on a daily basis. You should let the rest run down the stream so other families can eat. By doing this, the blessing keeps on coming. But, if you decide to put a net in and dam the river just for yourself, God will cut the blessing off.

You see, God never intended for a few people to own the world's goods. God's plan was to fill the earth with goods for us to live on so we can fulfill His plan for all of us to manage the earth and take care of it. To all of the people that think they own the earth and its contents, you are sadly mistaken. We don't own anything. We are only here to take care of the earth and share its goods with the poor.

Even if you are rich, and you can go and get yourself a $300 steak, and take four hours eating it, guess what? It's still not yours. The food in your stomach belongs to God too. So when God takes us from a place of lack and moves us into a place of plenty, we should have one thing on our minds – and that is seeking and searching out the needy so we can give back.

If God makes you rich, it will never be for you. You will just get to enjoy some of the benefits in the process. The real reason for Him making you rich is so you can help the needy. If you are rich, and are living good and people all around you are all hungry, you are not in line with the plan of God. When God makes you rich, you are supposed to be a distributor, a good man on the move in the field where people are hurting. And it's not like you have to look far to find hurting people.

I remember, not too long ago, we had an old living room completely full of old, worn out furniture. I thought that it was fit for one thing and one thing only, and that one thing was the garbage dump. So I loaded it up one day and went to the garbage dump. As soon as I started to unload the furniture, a little old lady who was very dirty came by and spoke to me. All of her clothes looked worse than the furniture that I was throwing away.

She said to me, “Please give that to me. Me and my grandchildren don't have anything to sit on. But, I don't have any way of getting it home.”

When I heard her say those things to me, I developed a soft spot in my heart for her and told her that I would take it home for her. Right then, I got my mind ready for my trip into a very bad neighborhood where anything could happen to me. She looked the part of a bad neighborhood, and she dressed like she came from a drug-infested, blown-out neighborhood. But what she told me next stopped me from judging people.

She looked at me and said, "I really thank you for helping me to move the furniture, but it won't take long because I live just right down the street."

When she said that, she knocked me off my feet and threw me for a loop. When I got there, I saw a very empty house. The only things that they had to sit on were raggedly pillows. I said to myself, surely this couldn't be happening in my neighborhood? The real truth of the matter is that it's happening all around us. So when God brings you into a place of plenty, make sure that there is no one under your nose crying and hungry and in need of daily medicine.

It is not all about you and your family. Almost anyone will feed their own. But, is your heart big enough to reach out and feed a stranger? Can you give away something you love that you know that you will never get back? When God brings us into a place of plenty, if we want to stay there, we have to start giving and let God be the provider.

If you just take care of "my" and "I," your well surely will run dry. God will never help you build yourself a personal warehouse of wealth. We have seen it over and over again. God blesses people and brings them into a place of plenty, but when they won't help anyone but themselves, God always moves the blessing away from them in some way or another. If we are not very watchful when we come into a place of plenty, instead of us spending the money, the money will spend us.

To keep this from happening, we must go full-time into outreach – which is simply helping other people with their needs by throwing out lifelines so someone else can climb up. In return, they can do the same thing so someone else can climb up. It is also about duplicating yourself when we come into a place of plenty. We should go full-time into the businesses of helping other people, instead of hoarding it all up for ourselves. The man that is willing to give it all away for God's sake will surely get it all back many times over.

No matter how much he gives away, he will always have more than he needs. It will be like a river of wealth running through and bubbling up in his life. It will break the backbone of the spirit of lack. We have to be like a boxer. We must always be ready to knock out the spirit of lack, and everything that associates with the spirit of lack, in people's lives.

How we do it is by giving and meeting needs in people's lives, both spiritual and natural. We must never become stagnant when we come into a place of plenty. Just like the prize fighter, we must exercise what we get until it grows big enough to make an impact in other people's lives when we fight. No matter where we fight, we shouldn't be any different.

When we come into a place of plenty, our life should be like a mighty fruit tree. We should bear so much fruit that everyone in the neighborhood can eat, and it should be plenty left over for the fowls of the air to eat. The reason why our fruit trees will get so big is by our giving, because every time we give, we prune our tree but God adds more to it.

If we only get $5, and God asks us to take it and feed it all to the poor, it will be easy to do. But when he brings you into a place of plenty, it may not be so easy for you. Like when you have $5,000,000 and he asks you to give all of away to the poor. Could you do it and trust God for more? Or, would you pack your bags and walk away from God?

When God brings you into a place of plenty, He will always be asking you to give it away so He can give more back to you. If you don't want God to ask you to give your wealth away, you better not accept wealth from Him in the first place. God's blessing is similar to a bakery assembly line. In the kitchen, millions of biscuits are wrapped, packaged and put on the line coming out of the kitchen and reaching outside where biscuits are being loaded into trucks.

If the loader stops loading them into trucks, and the trucks stop taking them away, the bakery will stop sending them out. Well, the same thing goes for God's blessings. If you stop sharing what you've been given and are not blessing other people in need, God will not continue to send out blessings to you. God wants His blessings to flow through you to other people in need.

He's not pouring just into your personal stockyard. So, when God brings you into a place of plenty, get ready to work and get ready to give. It is the only way that God does things. When you give, He gives. When you stop, He stops. But if you work for Him, and with Him, you will be in the realm of plenty forever.

Chapter 7

Our Future Pathway

Our future pathway must be laid out by God. We must follow Him across the goal line because He is the world's greatest running back. On our own, we have come upon the goal line of success many times in our lives, both spiritual and natural. We have failed almost every time! The reason why is because we keep leaving God out of our plans.

Failure will surely be a thing of the past if we get on the path that he had laid out for us. The pathway God has laid out for us is full of hope, love and justice. I have finally figured out from the past that our future will only be good if we let God lead us into it. For over 200 years, we have asked the man in charge to please give us our part in this life. But because he believes that God made the earth and put him in charge, and because he is selfish and greedy, his heart won't let him break bread fairly. He is a fool in his thinking.

God has never signed the deed of the earth over to anyone. Greedy and selfish men will always be around us. That's why we have to keep Jesus in all of our pathways. Anywhere we go, and any and every road we take, must be laid out for us by Him. Because prejudiced and racist men won't rid themselves of this troubling disease, we will always need His guidance and His power to go against the evil acts we encounter. Even today, ignorance and unfair racism is being passed down to our kids.

I just saw a new TV program where little kids were tested on the color of other little kids. It showed how they would respond to the expression of different facts that had been drawn on a poster or a card being shown to them. Now I believe that whoever drew these pictures, drew them to get the answer that they wanted. The test went like this: someone drew five kids and asked the kids to describe each of them and their facial expressions. There were two White girls on the left, a little Brown girl in the middle, and on the right were two little Black girls.

Now, the two White girls were drawn very pretty, and one of them had a smile on her face. The little Brown girl was drawn to look plain. The two Black girls were drawn so ugly and so Black that all you could see was the symbol of a face. Then they asked the group of kids to describe the facial expressions. There was one White boy and one White girl, one Black boy and one Black girl.

First, they were asked who was pretty. They all picked the smiling White girl. When they were asked who was fair looking, they all picked up the little Brown girl. When they all were asked who was smart, they all picked the other little White girl. Finally, when they were asked who was ugly, they all picked the little Black girls. When they were asked who was mean, they all picked the one of the Black girls. And when they were all asked who was dumb, they all picked the darkest little Black girl.

Now, we all know that a picture will be just what you draw it to be. I can draw a White woman so ugly that her own momma will reject her. I also I can draw a Black woman so pretty that men's tongue will fall out running after her. What I am saying is that we need to give the same test but reverse the kid's faces. The Black kids will win just like the White ones did. God doesn't want us to be a victim of that type of scoreboard.

In the future, we must lay out the test of life before everyone and make it plain so everyone can have a fair chance at winning. We must also be told why our pathway into the future must be God-based and enemy-proofed. When we travel in the future pathway, and stay in the lane that He has prepared for us, we won't fall. In obedience, there is safety. But when you are one step out of obedience, the world has a crack in the floor and they're waiting for you to fall through.

One pastor told me that when a man makes his ways right with God, they will automatically be all right with man whether man accepts it or not. But when we walk outside of the path that God has laid out for us, we will have the loser effect. This means that we step into the cracks of life that the world has always used to snare and get us off course. In the future, our love walk must be so strong and direct from God that when bad things are carried out against us, it will be like water on a duck's back and just run off.

But the enemy won't stop trying to get you off track because that is his job. All we have to do is to make sure that we are doing our job by staying on the path. He is not allowed to travel along with us. The enemy of our life is not permitted to come and play with us. That's why he is always inviting us to come and play with him. And the enemy of our life never stops studying and planning for our failure.

Now, he knows that he cannot get us as long as we are on the safety path God has prepared for us. That's why he constantly dangles world trophies in front of us. Our enemy is losing ground fast. After abusing us for years, we are no longer ignorant to his tricks. We now know that everything that we will ever need is in the pathway of life that God himself has laid out for us.

True friends do exist, along with every need met and unmet. In this pathway that God has laid out for us, there will never be a need for greed. The supplies will be so great that no man can ever run out of his part. So, there will never be a reason for greed. We will all look alike, be well fit, well dressed and well kept by God.

You see, when a man takes good care of his wife's needs, she can go to town or to the market place where another man sees her and admires her beauty, or even lay's out before her all of his treasures. But, she will remember her good husband that she has at home and loves. This will make her send her admirer on his way.

Well, the same thing goes for God. He knows who we have in Him and that another can't compare. We can't take the chance of losing him by entertaining another false god. A great wine maker will never mix his wine with another's cheaper brand. That's why we must stay in the lane that God has prepared for us. We know that everything the enemy has is counterfeit.

Only hope and love are found in the lane that God has prepared for us. We know that we have to stay in the safety lane that he has prepared for us because the enemy is very cunning and is always hanging around God's people. He doesn't see that God has a day planned to take the unfair part of his wealth and give it back to the poor. It’s just like when two men go out and equally kill a big bear. When the time comes to sell the hide, the selfish and greedy one, that thinks that God has put him in charge of mankind in the first place, will want the largest part of the money.

I feel sorry for that kind of person, because he has always thought that the right way to split and divide an apple was the two-in-one way. This means he gets two pieces where we get one piece. But since we teamed up with God, He put us on a winning path and in a lane of safety. We have our own whole apple to enjoy in this place where He has put us. Our blessings are super sized and safe.

If we have just enough for ourselves, we don't have enough. Yonder is the future. We can't just feed ourselves and think that it’s right. In the future, if our neighbor has a setback, we must sustain him until he can see about himself. On and in the path that God has laid out and prepared for us, a selfish heart won't survive.

On the future path, we won't entertain a greedy spirit and a selfish spirit. Those two spirits alone have tormented the world for a mighty long time. Slavery, and all of the suffering that it caused, came from a handful of men that were and still are full of selfishness and greed. They want everything God made, and they want it just for them – even if it takes killing millions to get it. They don't care about anyone other than themselves.

The one thing that they don't understand is how God works. God will let a greedy and selfish man steal and keep putting his unfair wealth up like a mountain. What he doesn't see is that in all of his unfair hard work and selfish planning, God is only waiting on them to finish stacking it up. Then He will take it from them and give it back to the poor and the just.

As we stay on and in the pathway to blessings, in the future, God will always come replenish us as a many times as it takes to keep us sustained and safe. Everything that was made or created has to be serviced by the one who made it or created it. If you go to the airport and watch an airplane take off, it leaves the ground with so much power that it seems like it's going to fly forever. But if you just go 500 miles to the next city's airport, you will see it back on the ground being serviced.

If man has enough sense to keep on servicing everything that he makes, what do you think about God? He will always be preparing our pathways of life. He keeps upgrading us to the fullness of life in the path that he has laid out for us. And the same enemy that had us down for hundreds of years, the one that never saw it coming, now knows that God himself is with us and is protecting and keeping us. That same enemy, that split everything three ways with us and got two parts when we only got one part, will see us when God gives us our part back. And that is a real truth.

Chapter 8

When Love Is Absent, Hate Will Run Rampage

From the beginning of this book up until this closing chapter, the subjects have been about people and some of the different events that have taken place or still may be going on. All of the negative events that were then or may be happening now are because the spirit of love was absent in them and may be still absent today.

The plantation owner wouldn't have abused his workers if he had the love of God in his life. The stay-home dad would get up off the couch and go to work if he loved his family. But because he has the lack of love in his life, he can't focus on taking care of his family. Because of the frame of mind that he is in, he sits and watches them struggle for basic needs.

So let me be very clear about the matter of love and hate. If a man possesses something that he doesn't love, then there is a good chance that he will abuse it, whether it be people or things. You see, hate doesn't love anybody but it wants to be with and in everybody. The spirit of hate will buffet a man, and toy with a man, for a spot or a place in his life.

Hate is like the pressure of the water in the sea, or a great ocean current, pushing and beating upon and against the wall of the ship of a man's life. If any little crack is torn in the hull by the pressure, water will rush in and consume him. Love, on the other hand, is different. Love will sit outside of your heart and wait until you open the door and invite him in. Then and only then will it come in.

We know that hate will come and box with us to get to a point where it can have a part in our life. And we know that it will beat upon the door of our hearts to try and get in no matter how long we ignore it. But then, we also know that we have to take a stand and push with even more pressure to keep hate out and love in. From now on we must talk in love and walk in love, in every area of our lives. We must be in love with mankind.

Let me make myself clear. People will move around in your life with their opinions about you. Today they may be very pleased with you, and tomorrow you say one little thing or do one little thing and they will be against you. Don't be concerned about what people say or think. The one that you are counting on is the one that is inside you, the one that runs the race in the first place.

Now that the next chapter of your life is upon you, many will gather with you at the starting line and say that they are with you. However, when you take on your new endeavor, be ready to go all the way by yourself if you need to. When you start out towards your new success, there will be some joining that bandwagon because they are nosey and want to see what's going on. There will be some joining in because they want to know, first hand, how bad you are going to fail.

Many different people will say that they are with you for various reasons. But true love for you will not be found among them. All of it will be extra weight that you must carry from day one in your new endeavor and quest for success. Because the presence of love is absent, they can't stay with you all the way. Now they have already seen you the way that you are, and some of them are the very ones that have counted you out in their hearts (and with their mouths) because of the lack of love in them.

My question to them is, how do you keep a man down who knows 1,000 different ways to get up? While you are engaged with your path to success, a great many of the ones that started out with you and said that they would be with you will be hearing of your success over and over. Then, jealousy sets in and anger sets in. One by one they begin to jump ship and team up in their hearts against you.

Because the love of God is present in you, and right from the beginning you counted the cost and prepared yourself to go all the way across the finish line, the lane that you are in and the goal line belong to you. Success will embrace you with arms wide open! And, the ones that don't finish the course (or cross the goal line with you) will think foolishly that they dumped you.

But the real truth is that God led them all away from you so they wouldn't be a hindrance to you. Everything in your life that can be shaken has been shaken. What you have left is strong and will remain, so enjoy the benefits of God that you have in your life. Stay in love with people.

By loving all humanity, you will surely stay in love with God. There are too many people trying to love God while hating people at the same time. But it won't work. We must first love each other. Only then can heaven and the things of God can be opened up to us and released to us.

It is a daily fight to keep the presence of God in our lives and the presence of hate out. But it is a fight worth fighting. The only way to keep hate out of our lives, and the presence of God in, is to go out of our way and love. We must love even when it is not popular to do so.

We don't want to be like any of the people going wrong. Like many of the people found on the pages of this book, we don't want to be kept from what is ours in this life. Neither do we want to keep other people from getting their part in this life. We don't want to be the men that love getting babies but hate taking care of them with love. And as far as I can see it, love has got to be our basis and reason for living. It's the only way we can ever truly live.

THE AUTHOR & BOOK

Duz Mack (Lee E. Mack, "Dr. Lee") is a native of Raymond, Mississippi, is a proud father of three children and grandfather of seven. Utilizing knowledge acquired during more than half a century of living and working, his debut, WAKE UP BLACK MAN: Your Future Is Calling You, addresses some rarely-discussed issues facing the Black-American man. With it, he hopes to impart ways to improve homes and communities worldwide.

"As I look around at our Black men, I decided somebody needed to say something about what was and is going on," the retired wireman said. "No one is going to give us anything. The time is now! We must be responsible men who fill ourselves with all the reinforcements we need so we can compete at a world-class level, and no one can ever say no to us again about jobs we are qualified for."

Duz contends that too many youths and adults are letting life slip away from them, mostly because no one ever alerted them about what is really happening around them. With WAKE UP BLACK MAN, he hopes to team with, and begin helping, current and future generations of Black males so they won't become or remain lost.

A graduate of Duley High School, during his spare time, Duz likes fishing, hunting, working, dancing and sight seeing. He also enjoys spending time cooking and barbecuing at family gatherings and fish frys. His current projects include writing folk songs and completing other books. His second release, the title of which is presently being withheld, is expected to become available to the general public during 2010 as well.

(bepublished.biz, toni_crump@buildingfuturegenerations.org)

THE CONTRIBUTORS

Editor – **Toni Crump**, a native of Clinton, Mississippi, is presently completing her senior year at Mississippi College. Her professional experience includes creating and updating legal documents, handling business correspondence, and assisting with special projects. Her future plans are to use her administrative and organizational skills to succeed as an entrepreneur. Among Toni's most prized achievements to date is her being able to assist her grandfather, Duz Mack, with fulfilling his dream of authorship by publishing his debut **WAKE UP BLACK MAN: Your Future Is Calling You**. *(toni_crump@buildingfuturegenerations.org)*

Editor/Cover Designer – **Mylia Tiye Mal Jaza** (Dr. Mary Jefferson) is a Texippian and Chicago entrepreneur. Two of her 10 books were republished works written by ancestors of hers – The Facts Of Reconstruction by John R. Lynch and The Old Negro And The New Negro by T. Leroy Jefferson, M.D. Her books ranged in content from poetry/prose to film/television scripts: Life Is Beautiful: La Vita E Bella, Life Is Beautiful: La Vita Es Hermosa, Seen In Other Words, Plea For Peace, All For Show, Scientific Evidence God Exists, Elegies Of A Goddess, and And. The artist/vocalist has also helped communities by cleaning highways, feeding the homeless, gifting shelters/nursing homes, and giving youth school supplies. *(mari@bepublished.org)*

www.ingramcontent.com/pod-product-compliance
Ingram Content Group UK Ltd.
Pitfield, Milton Keynes, MK11 3LW, UK
UKHW020237250726
13967UKWH00001B/426

9 780557 678532